IN CHRIST

THE WONDERS OF CHRIST IN YOU

RYAN AITKEN

IN CHRIST

THE WONDERS OF CHRIST IN YOU

RYAN AITKEN

FOREWORD

I first caught sight of Ryan Aitken at a Healing Rooms Training I taught in 2012. I was drawn to the glow of his countenance, and the joy and underlying mischief I saw there. He had just returned to Bethel Church from South Africa with his lovely wife Audrey and wanted to get involved in our Healing Rooms.

I began to observe the strong commitment on Ryan's life both for healing breakthrough and for the presence of God. We connected. The Healing Rooms is a divine experiment that entails generating a united heart and an atmosphere that attracts Heaven, which then allows Heaven to break out in a myriad of ways, changing people, their symptoms, sicknesses and pain. People encounter God's love and healing happens. Sometimes we pray...

Ryan played well in this environment. He soon became a leader in stimulating change, which then allowed ailing people to dislodge from their familiar conditions and receive the healing that pours eternally from the cross of Jesus. I noticed he also helped our ministry teams dislodge from the dense muck of religious prayers to move into more freedom and success. So I asked him to intern with me. With Audrey and three other interns we met every Friday to feast on breakfast and discuss life and issues, ask questions and search out answers, sing and pray together and mostly love each other and savor the very present God in our midst. We traveled across Switzerland and France with a team of students ministering on streets, in coffeehouses, healing rooms, churches and conferences. I got to see Ryan up close and feel his passion, hunger, anointing and convictions. Ryan is the real deal. He is anointed and gifted, but also searches out truth and answers in scripture and by asking great questions. I love his commitment to see the things God promises become reality. I love that he's always looking for new ways and better ways to bring the benefits of the Kingdom of Heaven into this realm for the benefit of many.

Here's Ryan's first book. Enjoy the revelation of the "simplicity that is in Christ."

Chuck Parry
Bethel Church - Associate Director Healing Rooms
www.chuckparry.com

ENDORSEMENTS

Ryan Aitken is not just one who pursues revival, he is one living revival. Ryan life has been transformed by the love and power of the Holy Spirit. This book is an overflow of Ryan's radical love for Jesus and, therefore, acts as an invitation for each of us to accept all that Christ has made available. "In Christ" reveals God's heart to, not just rescue His people, but to empower them and make them new creations by putting His very Spirit inside of them. These pages will not only inspire you but they will also provide a strong Biblical foundation that reveals the beauty of God's plan for His people, and teaches us very practical tools to help us walk in this transforming power. Open your heart and let the truth of Christ's love change you forever.

Joaquin Evans
Bethel Church - Pastoral Team
Presence Pursuit Ministries - Founder
www.presencepursuit.com

Ryan has written an incredible book challenging and calling all Christians into greater levels of intimacy, hearing God's voice, and miracle breakthrough power. As you read this book, you will be challenged and encouraged in your identity. It is written with a solid biblical foundation and full of Ryan's supernatural experiences. I would challenge all Christians that want to receive an upgrade from heaven to indulge in this book.

Chris Gore
Bethel Church - Director Healing Rooms
Author, Walking in Supernatural Healing Power

Ryan Aitken's desire to know and serve the Lord centers around his experience involving his own journey where he encounters the Lord.   After this encounter he has greater insights into the spiritual battle, the attributes of God and God's plans of Christ within us.   The author also makes clear the practical work of "the Helper."   Much of the book is helpful for spiritual devotions and for small group Bible studies and teaching such as the natural senses and the spiritual senses.   If you desire revival, Ryan's book will challenge the reader to experience "the wonders of Christ in you."

Dr. Rev. William Wilbur
Gamboa Union Church - Pastor
Rep. of Panama

Ryan's personal journey of truly knowing Jesus is an inspiration that will captivate all who read this. I was encouraged and motivated to 'know' Jesus at even deeper levels. A thrilling must read for all who truly want to develop a clear identity in Jesus!

Les Coombs
Bethel Church - Healing Rooms Pastor

This book is dedicated to my beautiful wife Audrey.

I am so thankful for all your constant support and encouragement. I am so grateful that I found a partner that lives for eternity, for the day when we stand before our Father in heaven. One that lives to please God in everything.

To contact the author about speaking at your conference or church, please go to
www.spiritofrevival.com

Editor: Sarah Wind
Associate Editor: Annette Carson
Designer: Simeon Jansen
Formatter: Simeon Jansen
Artwork: Audrey Aitken

ISBN 978-1-942306-76-4
Printed in the United States of America

OTHER BOOKS BY RYAN AITKEN
Keys to Healing (Manual)

TABLE OF CONTENTS

Introduction   15

1 Looking in the Mirror   17

2 Master Plan of God   27

3 Christ in You   39

4 The Voice of God   51

5 Spiritual Senses 1-2   65

6 Spiritual Senses 3-5   87

7 The Heart of God   99

INTRODUCTION

Everything God does is with a stroke of divine brilliance.

Today the church is coming into a greater understanding of her authority and uniqueness.

She is awaking to the realization that she is not the *victim* but the *victor*.

Our journey as the bride of Christ into all that God has done for us is an enthralling rollercoaster of discovery.

God is sending forth an invitation into a deeper revelation of who He is and what He has done for us.

```
┌─────────┐
│         │
│    1    │
│         │
└─────────┘
```

LOOKING IN THE MIRROR

WHAT DO YOU LOOK LIKE?

People across the world every day wake up in the morning and before they leave their house they look in the mirror. What are they looking for? They are, in a sense looking for faults. They are looking to see if there is sleep in their eyes, hair sticking up, or pimples that have formed. People want to look good and presentable. If for example someone has sleep hair and they know it, their hair will plague their mind for the rest of their day as they relentlessly try and get their hair in place. So the main reason people have mirrors in their bathrooms is to see what blemishes in their appearance exist that need to be fixed.

The traditional teaching in the body of Christ is that God has given the mirror, or the Word of God, so that He can show us all the blemishes in our lives. We are taught to look inward and search for all the secret unknown sins in our lives. We come to church to be shown all our faults and failures, so hopefully through guilt and manipulation we might change for the better. For the most part, if change happens, it's by self-modification, energized by guilt and condemnation. The Lord's help and grace is left out, and if there is change, it happens by the sweat of our brow.

WHO YOU ARE ON THE INSIDE

But this was never God's intent. Looking in the mirror of God's Word was meant to remind us how beautiful we are. In Christianity, the renewing of the mind is really all about looking in the mirror of God's Word. God's Word is meant to lift us up into a new realm of thinking. So that, our mind is renewed to the place of realizing God's perfection in us.

"and you are <u>complete in Him,</u> who is the head of all principality and power."

~ Col 2:10

18

Looking in the mirror of God's Word is not an inward gazing at all the faults and blemishes in our lives. It is not looking for hidden sins that we feel need to be confessed. Rather, looking in the mirror is looking in at the perfection of Christ's work in us. In essence, while looking in the mirror we are looking at the completed work of the cross. We are intuitively designed to become the thing that we see before us. Why? Because, how we see and think about ourselves will determine what we become.

"As he thinketh in his heart, so is he"

~Prov. 23:7

While Jesus was talking to Jews under the law, He said, "The food that you put into your mouth doesn't make you unclean and unfit to worship God. The bad words that come out of your mouth are what make you unclean" (Matt. 15:11). What was He saying? He was saying that the realities of an inwardly unclean heart will manifest outwardly in unclean language and behavior.

I know a man who owned a very successful million-dollar business. Unfortunately because of a number of factors he lost it all. The amazing thing is that in a very short time he started a new company that became a successful million-dollar business. Now was this just a fluke or is there something to this? There are many businessmen and women who work very hard but never get to the stage of having such a successful business. But because this man was a millionaire on the inside, it was just a matter of time for it to manifest on the outside again.

Who you are as a person is directly manifested by who you think you are. If you think you are a sinner you will sin; if you think you are pure you will walk in purity. How we think about ourselves will affect our walk with God negatively or positively. Crazy as it might sound, a son who had a bad father often mimics his father when he has children even though he vowed to never to become like him. Why does this happen? This happens because the son filled his thoughts with who he vowed he would never become, and he did not fill his thoughts with becoming a great father. In the end because the son filled his thoughts on what he didn't want to become, he became what he didn't want to become.

Like it or not, who you are right now is the sum total of your thoughts. If you have a desire to change the world and become a revivalist, then you need to change the way you think. You won't become a world changer unless you think like a world changer.

TRANSFORMED BY WHO WE BEHOLD

This is why the prophetic is so important in the lives of Christians. When an accurate word is given to an individual, there is a release of the way God sees them and their ability. If the individual receives this word, there is a renewing of the way they think and their thought pattern is changed to the mind of Christ. Now, because this individual is thinking the way God thinks, there will be a release of grace to become what God said they could become. All that we could possibly want to become in God is propelled by us gazing on the Lord and thinking the thoughts of God.

"But we all, with unveiled face beholding as in a mirror the glory of the Lord, are being transformed into the same image from glory to glory, just as by the Spirit of the Lord."

~ 2 Cor. 3:18

We become the one we behold before us. When we gaze upon Him, the glorious one, we become glorious. Ultimately, we become the one we worship. This is why I believe God's heart is that we never worship idols. Whatever we fix our gaze and attention on we become.

We are not designed to look at ourselves and all of our failures; we are designed to look at Him. As we gaze intently at Him, we are transformed into who He is. The longer we gaze, the more we are gloriously transformed into His likeness. Our outward gaze will become our inward reality.

"But we know that when Christ appears, we shall be like him, for we shall see him as he is"

~ 1 John 3:2

When we see Him in all His magnificence, something happens inside of us. Gazing at the Great One stirs in our own heart's greatness because we are made in the image of greatness. When we see the triumphant one, we receive courage to fight another day. When we see the loving one, we have compassion for the weak and feeble.

Our whole lives are a poem, a worship set to God. The worshippers that God wants are worshippers that "will worship the Father in the Spirit and in truth" (John 4:23). All true worship is birthed out of the revelation of who He is.

GROWING IN FAITH BY BEHOLDING

What first drew me to Jesus was how incredibly good and loving He is. My encounter with His love caused me to have faith in Him, and in the revelation of His goodness, I gave my all to Him. In reality the kindness of God led me to repentance (Rom. 2:4).

There is a desperate need for greater levels of faith in the body of Christ. But I have learned that looking inward to try and increase my own faith never really worked. All I felt was an increased feeling of discouragement and hopelessness.

The secret of Christianity is this: When we have our eyes fixed on the faithful one, our hearts are then infused with faith. Whether we are in need of a financial miracle, a physical miracle, or a relational miracle, we are called to look at the faithful one. When we look at Him in all His majesty there is an explosion of faith inside of us. In the revelation of His faithfulness we receive the faith of Christ. He is after all, "the author and perfecter of faith" (Heb. 12:2).

Satan knows if he can get our eyes off of God and onto our failures, he will set us on a downward spiral of destruction. When God looks down on one of His children, He sees us through the lenses of who we are going to become. He is not filled with anxiety about where we are, because He sees the beginning from the end. As the Apostle Paul said,

"He who began a good work in you will carry it on to completion until the day of Christ Jesus."

~ Phil. 1:6

What if the secret of every breakthrough, is just as simple as getting lost in Jesus and having a greater revelation of who He is? The revelation of who Christ is and who you are in Christ will break every yoke of the devil. Our job is to get lost in Jesus.

GOD'S GENERAL

John G. Lake is one of my personal heroes and he is a great example of what it looks like to be lost in Jesus. During his lifetime he left a heritage of over 1,000 written sermons, over 100,000 converts (in Africa alone), and countless miracles. He established "Lake's Divine Healing Institute" in Spokane, Washington, which produced so many supernatural healings that the United States government labeled Spokane "the healthiest city in the world." In my personal opinion, the teachings of Mr. Lake are just as applicable today as they were 100 years ago. He was a man who had an incredible understanding of the reality of Christ's incarnation in the soul of a man. While reading about his life it was interesting to note one of his daily disciplines:

> As he got dressed each day, Lake made a habit of walking over to his mirror, pointing to it as if to another person and saying: "God lives in that man in that suit of clothes. And where that suit of clothes goes, God goes."
>
> ~ John G. Lake

When we get to the place of a deep revelation of who it is that lives inside of us, we will in essence become the hands and feet of Jesus on this earth. What we are called to do is to take a good look at Jesus, then stare intently in the mirror at the one who lives inside us. By beholding Him in this manner we will be transformed from glory to glory.

2

MASTER PLAN OF GOD

THE ATTRIBUTES OF GOD

God is omniscient, which means He is all knowing. In all of existence there is not one bit of information that God does not intuitively know. In Himself, God embodies all wisdom and knowledge. All knowledge we may discover was found in Him before time began. All His attributes are interlinked with each other. For Him to be all knowing (omniscient) means he must also be everywhere (omnipresent), which means He must also be all powerful (omnipotent) and the sovereign ruler of all things. So in all this we know that when God comes up with a plan for humanity, it is no ordinary plan; it is the creator's master plan. This master plan is flawless and perfect. It is a complete stroke of brilliance created by I Am Himself.

MASTER PLAN OF GOD: THE GLORIOUS GOSPEL

This master plan of God has always been the gospel (the good news). And I believe what most of the church thinks the gospel is, has little comparison to what God intended it to be.

His gospel is a stumbling block to the religious, and complete foolishness to the world's way of thinking (1 Cor. 1:23-24). This master plan of God is so far beyond humanity's typical way of thinking that Jesus said in order to grasp it we must take on the mindset and viewpoint of a child (Matt. 18:3). The gospel is not just a hopeful ticket to heaven as we eagerly await the return of Christ to escape this despicable place called earth.

It's even greater than walking into the reality of the forgiveness of sins and healing. The word for salvation in Greek is "sozo," meaning forgiveness of sins, healing (of whole being), deliverance, and prosperity. The salvation of God has to do with restoring us and dealing with the realities of living in a fallen world. The reality of this salvation is powerful in of itself, but I believe it goes even deeper than this.

God takes us from being defeated individuals to children of the most high.

"For if, by the trespass of the one man, death reigned through that one man, how much more will those who receive God's abundant provision of grace and of the gift of righteousness reign in life through the one man, Jesus Christ"

~ Rom. 5:17

In Col. 1:25-27 we see Paul writing about the master plan of God:

"So that I might fully carry out the preaching of the word of God, that is, the mystery which has been hidden from the past ages and generations, but has now been manifested to His saints, to whom God willed to make known what is the riches of the glory of this mystery among the Gentiles, which is Christ in you, the hope of glory."

UNVEILING THE MASTER PLAN

Wow! The master plan of God, the mystery hidden for ages, is Christ in us! For ages and generations, since the dawn of creation, angels, prophets, and men of God have looked for the master plan of God to no avail. I believe even the mightiest of angels had no idea what God had up His sleeve for mankind (1 Pet.

1:12). Now through the knowledge of Jesus Christ, it is revealed to us. Paul calls it the secret plan of God; it's the mystery of heaven, the Father's secret that He has now revealed to His children. Since the fall, God had this sneaky master plan. Through the completed work on the cross and the glorification of His Son, this plan is now set in motion.

"All who declare that Jesus is the Son of God have God living in them, and they live in God"

~ 1 John 4:15

We now realize that the work of Jesus on the cross was not just a massive repair job for humanity, but rather an upgrade, and an astonishing upgrade at that! "If anyone is in Christ, he is a new creature; the old things passed away; behold, new things have come" (2 Cor. 5:17). The word "new creature" means in the original Greek, "Something that has never embraced this world before."

"We are all together new, aliens on this earth, and citizens of another world"

~ 1 Pet. 2:11

Imagine I was an old rusted 1985 Ford truck that could barely make it to the gas station. I needed to be repaired badly, so I was driven to the auto repair shop so that Jesus could fix me. But in a moment of realization of who Jesus is, I was transformed by the power of the gospel. This transformation was not from a rusty truck to a brand new economical car. This would be amazing by itself. The gospel's upgrade is far greater, in an instant I was changed from a rusty truck to a brand new top of the line jet. I thought that I was going to be patched up by Him, but instead I was changed into a totally new creation! That's what happens when we become followers of Jesus. He takes us from the guttermost to the uttermost!

AS HE IS, NOT AS HE WAS

In 1 John 4:17 we hear probably one of the most incredible statements the Bible has to offer, "as He is, so are we in this world". Notice, it does not say, "as He was." It says, "as He is." If we walked like Jesus walked on this earth, that would be amazing enough by itself. Imagine raising the dead, healing cripples, walking on water, and commanding weather. But God had a greater plan, a secret masterful plan.

The Holy Spirit was sent onto this earth, not to transform us into who Jesus was, but into who He is right at this very moment. This is why the Father did not send the Holy Spirit at the cross, or even after the resurrection. He only sent the Holy Spirit once Jesus was in His glorified state.

At this moment, Jesus sits far above every rule power and dominion (Eph. 1:20-21; Mark 16:19). He sits in triumph over His enemies. At this very moment He is clothed in a robe reaching to his feet. His head and his hair are white like wool and His eyes are like flames of fire. His voice sounds like a trumpet and out of His mouth comes a sharp double-edged sword. His face looks like the sun in all its brilliance (Rev. 1:13-16). Jesus sits in heaven and has supreme power over all things. He sits in victory over every sin, sickness, and demonic oppression. We are found in Him, seated in Christ (Eph. 2:6). We have been co-crucified, co-buried, and co-risen with Christ (Gal. 2:20; Col. 2:12, 3:1; Rom. 6:4). We are victorious right now, because we are one with the victorious one! In the Spirit this is who we are.

OUR NEED FOR HOLY SPIRIT

This is why Jesus said, "It is better for you that I go away. If I do not go, the Helper will not come to you. If I go, I will send Him to you" (John 16:7). I think this is an amazing statement. If you had a choice today, between having Jesus walk around or the Holy Spirit, which would you choose? Jesus feels that it would be better to have the Holy Spirit. Why? Because the Holy Spirit will transform you into who Jesus is right now.

Jesus said,

"Truly, truly I say to you, he who believes in me, the works that I do, he will do also, and greater works than these he will do; because I go to the Father"

~ John 14:12

The Holy Spirit will not rest until He manifests the reality of Christ in you, consuming you from the inside out. He wants to explode and burn in every part of you, manifesting Jesus to a dying and broken world.

THE EARLY CHRISTIANS

The Holy Spirit's plan has always been for us as Christians to become like Jesus on this earth. In Acts 11:26 it mentions that the disciples in Antioch were the first to be called Christians. The term "Christian" means Christ-like. In my earlier years of Christianity, I used to think that these disciples were the first to be called Christians because their purity level was similar to what Jesus displayed. I believe this to be true, but I do not believe this is the only reason. I believe they so demonstrated the love and power of Jesus that outsiders began to say that they looked and acted like Him. Jesus walked in incredible purity. But He also cast out demons, raised the dead, cleansed lepers, and healed the multitudes.

It's interesting to note that the church in Antioch had been receiving incredible teaching by Paul and

Barnabas about the gospel of Jesus. For a full year, they were taught the true gospel, and because of this they began to manifest Christ in them to the world around them. The people of Antioch witnessed that the lives of these believers were so similar to the life of Jesus, not just in purity but also in power, that they were led to call them Christians (Christ like). We are on a journey of discovering who we really are, and when the Spirit of revelation reveals this, we will manifest Jesus in all His brilliance to the world around us.

GOD'S INTENTION FOR THE GOSPEL

So what is the master plan of God? It is simply the reality of Christ inside of us! The ingenious plan of God is that God would raise up an entire army, a nation of Christ-like people that would take over the world, in world domination. Jesus was limited by time and space while He lived on the earth. All His endeavors on the earth led to the place where He would raise duplicates of Himself after He rose from the dead and the Holy Spirit came. Jesus would come into the lives of men and women, have His habitation inside of them, and transform them into His likeness in both purity and power, just like the early Antioch disciples. With this in mind God would, through the lives of His children, plunder the enemy's camp and take over the world.

My Own Journey

In my own life I had a powerful encounter with Jesus that would forever mark who I am. While I was living in Hong Kong, I developed a particular hunger in my spirit to see the Lord. I laid hold of the Scripture where Jesus says, "The one who loves me will be loved by my Father, and I too will love them and show myself to them" (John 14:21). This Scripture became a continuous prayer in my life. During that time I received a prophetic word that said I would see the Lord before the year ended. Months later I found myself in a prayer meeting listening to a minister talk about the reality of our union with Christ and the Father. After he spoke we had a time of worship and I was immediately taken to an incredible place of intimacy with the Lord.

I was catapulted into a vision and I saw an Arabic man dressed like a rabbi. The person in the vision was a bit unclear because he was standing at least 30 feet away. I thought that this was possibly one of the heroes of the faith. At this point I asked the Lord, "Who is this?" As soon as I asked this, in an instant the Lord Jesus stood before me. I was completely captured by His majestic presence. He carried such authority and power that I knew every knee must bow before Him. I fell as though dead on the floor, and the riveting fire of God blazed through my body. I wept and wailed as I was undone by His majesty. The conquest of heaven saturated every fiber in my being. In that place God spoke to me and said, "This is who you are in the Spirit. I live in you!"

For days I could barely speak, choking under the remembrance of the encounter. In all this, the realization of Him who lives in me became even more real. I am the incarnation of Christ on this earth. I have been united with Christ in His death, burial, and resurrection. My spirit man has the same effect on demons, sickness, and creation as Jesus has. When I look in the mirror I do not only look at Ryan, but I look at Christ in me.

Interestingly when the seven sons of Sceva tried casting out a particular demon the demon replied:

"'Jesus I know, and Paul I know about, but who are you?' Then the man who had the evil spirit jumped on them and overpowered them all. He gave them such a beating that they ran out of the house naked and bleeding"

~ Acts 19:15-16

I believe that the demonic will only submit to the one who has all power and authority, who is Jesus. Paul was not just recognized in the earthly realm, but also in the unseen spirit realm. He was known as one that brought havoc in the demonic realm. He was known and feared not because he was special, but because of the all-powerful one who lived inside him.

Paul realized this and He ministered out of the authority and power of Jesus inside him. Paul said,

"I have been crucified with Christ and I no longer live, but Christ lives in me. The life I now live in the body, I live by faith in the Son of God, who loved me and gave himself for me."

~ Gal. 2:20

REVIVAL IS HERE AND NOW

Religion always wants to put a delay on the promises of God, saying that they are for another dispensation. The Bible clearly states that,

"In the last days, the mountain of the Lord's house will be the highest of all – the most important place on earth. It will be raised above the other hills, and people from all over the world will stream there to worship."

~ Isaiah 2:2

"The earth will be filled with the knowledge of the glory of the Lord as the waters cover the sea."

~ Hab. 2:14

It's time for us to live out this verse:
"Arise, shine; for your light has come, and the glory of the Lord has risen upon you."

~ Isaiah 60:1

This light is Jesus, the light of the world. Revival has always been here. It is not in the distant future; it is inside of us. Jesus is all the revival we need. Let us arise and shine, and as we arise the King of glory will arise through our lives. From this place the world around us will be changed. Saints, let us gaze into the mirror and see the perfection of Christ in us. Let us see the one who stands before us.

3

CHRIST IN YOU

REIGNING IN CHRIST

The world is awakening to that marvelous truth, that Christ is not in the heavens only, nor in the atmosphere only, but Christ is IN YOU. I feel in my heart the great need for believers around the world to come to a greater realization of the one who lives inside of them. Unfortunately,

many people accept Jesus into their hearts, but in their mind because of their warped view of who Jesus is, their understanding of the indwelling of Christ has little value to them. If you read through the Gospels you will see that we have not received a baby Jesus, or a suffering Jesus, or a blonde haired blue eyed Jesus. We have received the King of Kings and The Lord of Lords.
(Lake 91)

We have received in ourselves the first and the last, the living one who is alive forevermore, who has the keys of death and hades (Rev. 1:17-18). Our perception of who He is must change and our minds must be renewed to see the reality of who He really is in us.

THE WONDER OF UNION

When Jesus Christ made His home in us, the greatest miracle the world has ever known took place. Jesus, in whom the fullness of the Godhead dwelt in, now lives in us (Col. 2:9-10). This is the same Jesus that walked the earth and lived life having the Holy Spirit without measure (John 3:34).

Jesus said,
"Do you not believe that I am in the Father, and the Father is in Me? The words that I say to you I do not speak on My own initiative, but the Father abiding in Me does His works"

~ John 14:10

In essence, because we are now one with Jesus, we have the triune God making His home in us. We are the temple of the Holy Spirit (1 Cor. 6:19), we have Christ in us (Col. 1:27), and because He is one with Father we are one with the Father. The very Spirit of God rises up in us and cries out "Abba, Father" (Rom. 8:15). Presently we are being sandwiched in the Godhead's full embrace. We are being wrapped in the love of the Father, Son, and Holy Spirit. We live in a perpetual encounter with God's love, peace, and joy. The Bible says that all God's delight is towards us, and He calls us His excellent ones (Ps. 16:3).

LIVING OUT YOUR POSITION

So where is Jesus seated right now? The Bible says He is seated at the right hand of the Father in heavenly places (Matt. 26:64; Mark 14:62, 16:19; Acts 2:33-34, Rom. 8:34; Eph. 1:20). In reality all of heaven lives in us. Jesus said, "The Kingdom of heaven is within you" (Luke 17:21). With both heaven and Jesus inside of us we are able to arise and shine (Isa. 60:1).

We are the seed of God, created in Him before time began as His offspring (1 John 4:9). The thing about a seed is, it has in itself the ability to become the tree it came from. It grows into the same exact type of tree that it came from! We also, grow in the likeness of Christ. This concept is portrayed throughout scripture, the imagery of us being like trees.

"The righteous will flourish like a palm tree, they will grow like a cedar of Lebanon."

~ Psalms 92:12

"They will be called oaks of righteousness, a planting of the LORD for the display of his splendor."

~ Isaiah 61:3b

Daily, as we meditate on the word of God, as we gaze upon Jesus, we are transformed. We grow and mature as believers, growing into the fullness of Christ. Becoming like Him, that we "may grow up into him in all things." (Eph. 4:15)

We are divinely made in God's image and likeness (Gen. 1:26). Although we will never become God, in ourselves we carry the very nature of God, the DNA of heaven.

"In Him we live and move and have our being, as also some of your own poets have said, 'For we are also His offspring.'"

~ Acts 17:28

We are the habitation of God here on the earth, and He has made His home in us (1 John 4:15). We have been united with the Lord and are one with Him in spirit (1 Cor. 6:17). We are seated in Him in heavenly places, in victorious union with Him, who made a public spectacle of the devil, disarming him at the cross (Col. 2:15).

Being one with Christ can be compared to being Siamese twins with Him, sharing the same heart and blood. His blood knows no record of sin, sickness, or disease. Having become co-equal heirs with Him (Rom. 8:17), we now walk with the same access to the Father as Jesus has. Because we have been joined together with Him, we have received the heart and mind of Christ, the resurrection power of Christ, and the faith and authority of Christ. We are inseparable from Him, and because of this, He will not withdraw His love from us.

"I am convinced neither death nor life, neither angels nor demons, neither the present nor the future, nor any powers, neither height nor depth, nor anything else in all creation, will be able to

separate us from the love of God that is in Christ Jesus our Lord"

~ Rom. 8:38-39

ELIMINATING PERFORMANCE MINDSETS

For many years I lived with a performance mindset. Before I would minister to people I would spend hours with God to get power, joy, and peace. My mindset was a lack mindset. I envisioned God giving me something that I didn't have. I would strive in prayer to earn the blessings of God through self effort.

One day I realized that I wanted to spend time with Him, not to try get something from Him for ministering to people, but just to be with Him. I realized that my first ministry should always be to the Lord, and then from that place I should minister to those around me. I meditated on the reality that I'm one with Him and that He is not a God that is far off but Immanuel, "God with us" (Matt. 1:23).

As I started to do this all the striving left, and I began to enjoy the revelation of God's habitation in me. You see I do not need to try to get plugged in to God; I am plugged in already. I do not need to work for God, but I get to work with Him.

JESUS' INCREDIBLE STATEMENT

"And the glory which You gave Me I have given them, that they may be one just as We are one: I in them, and You in Me"

~ John 17:22-23

We now share in an inheritance of the Father's glory through Jesus. This glory is revealed by Jesus Christ in us. It is "Christ in you the hope of glory" (Col. 1:27). Jesus demonstrated the indwelling glory of the Father when He went up to the Mount of Transfiguration.

"Jesus took Peter, James, and John, and led them up on a high mountain apart by themselves; and He was transfigured before them. His clothes became shining, exceedingly white, like snow, such as no launderer on earth can whiten them"

~ Mark 9:2-3

Right before the disciples' eyes the inward dwelling glory of the Father was released. Every molecule in Jesus' body was supercharged with divine glory, to the extent that His clothes began to self-illuminate with that radiant glory. As Jesus came down the mountain the Bible says,

45

"immediately all the crowd, when they saw Jesus [returning from the holy mount, His face and person yet glistening], they were greatly amazed and ran up to Him [and] greeted Him"

~ Mark 9:15

This type of transfiguration became a relatively common occurrence for the early church. Stephen's face radiated like the appearance of an angel while he received false accusations (Acts 6:8-15). Many other church disciples had similar occurrences like Princess Elizabeth of Hungary (1207-1231). It is said that her very countenance would give forth rays of light after she prayed. Many of the saints of old are depicted as having halos above their heads, these halos in ancient times represented the glory of God.

HIS GLORY WITHIN

We have the very glory of Jesus hidden in us. "We possess this precious treasure [the divine Light of the Gospel] in [frail, human] vessels of earth" (2 Cor. 4:7). Our mortal bodies are weak but in them resides the very glory of heaven, the light of the gospel. Heaven itself has no need for light from the moon or the sun, because the radiant glory of Jesus illuminates heaven. The illumination of Christ in me, if released, creates a transfiguration and a radiance of His glory in and through me.

Then we understand what Christ's redemption means. It is bringing out of Christ IN YOU, until Christ in you is the One manifest-manifest through your eyes just as God was manifest through the eyes of Jesus, manifest through your touch just as God was manifest through Jesus. It is not a power nor a life separate from yourself but, two lives made one, two natures co-joined, two minds operating as one, Christ in YOU.
(Lake 93-94)

In 2 Corinthians 6:16 we read,

"I will dwell in them and walk among them. I will be their God, and they shall be My people."

BACK TO THE GARDEN

The reality of this indwelling of Christ, in the sons of man affects everything around us. If we go back to the Garden of Eden before man fell from glory, we see God's original intent for man. His intent for us from the start was to subdue the earth and rule it (Gen. 1:26-28). Man was given the authority to govern and lead the earth, to care for and protect it. Adam went around giving names to everything found in the garden, maintaining everything in godly order. Creation was free under the stewardship of man. Adam in a sense was a god on the earth. That's why the Bible says, "you are gods, and all of you are sons of the Most High" (Ps. 82:6). We are not gods in the sense of divinity but in the sense of rulership.

"The heavens belong to the Lord, but he has given the earth to all humanity".

~ Psalm 115:16

Before the fall, creation lived in glorious freedom, everything vibrated with the resplendent glory of the Lord. There was no law of sin and death at work on the earth and everything lived and moved in perfect harmony. One can only imagine what the earth looked like and smelled like as creation freely expressed itself.

Because of the fall, creation was placed under a curse subjecting it to frustration, bondage, and decay. It has shrunk back in its expressions of itself, and today the beauty of creation that is all around us is only a fragment of its true grandeur. Creation now groans and aches for freedom.

CREATION AWAITS OUR ARISING

"For [even the whole] creation (all nature) waits expectantly and longs earnestly for God's sons to be made known [waits for the revealing, the disclosing of their sonship]"

~ Rom. 8:19

Creation longs for us to walk in our true identity. When we arise and shine, there is a release of glory that will liberate creation itself. It's our job as children of God to rise up, to govern and to lead creation into its glorious freedom. That's why I believe the Lord has commissioned us to, "Go into all the world and preach the gospel to all creation" (Mark 16:15).

4

THE VOICE OF GOD

HEARING GOD FOR OURSELVES

For many, the voice of God has been a confusing area of Christianity. We all have big and small decisions to make continuously. In the process of making decisions we either embrace the voice of God or disdain it, casting it away as irrational internal imaginations and carrying on with our humanistic decision making. When looking at the written Word of God we see the incredible power of God's spoken Word, and the importance it has in our lives.

CONFIDENCE IN HEARING HIM

Hearing God speak into a situation changes everything. For a Christian, hearing God's voice is the most important thing they could do. It is natural for Christians to hear God's voice because God has designed us to both hear and follow His voice.

"My sheep hear my voice, and I know them, and they follow me."

~ John 10:27

"Morning by morning he awakens; he awakens my ear to hear as those who are taught."

~ Isa. 50:4

A lot of teaching is going around about hearing God's voice. Some teaching sends the message that it's hard to hear His voice and you have to work really hard to hear it. We often hear stories of people who needed to hear God on an urgent situation so they went into the prayer closet and fasted for many days to hear Him speak.

The truth is that God is always speaking. He is the living Word. As soon as we are trying with our self-effort to earn the ability to hear His voice, we both miss His grace and voice. When we are in rest and peace we are able to listen, not with our heads, but with our hearts, and hear what the Spirit of God is saying to us.

I once heard the Vicar of Baghdad share his amazing perspective on hearing the voice of God. He said that when he needs to hear God on a situation, he asks God and then waits no more than two minutes. He believes that God will speak to him during this time.

Our expectancy of how long it takes to hear God's voice will mostly determine when we will start to listen. If I expect Him to only speak at the end of a week of fasting and prayer, then that is when I will hear Him speak. If I believe I am a friend of God, and friends have conversations with God, then I will have an expectancy to hear Him speak quickly. I do not intend to negate the reality and discipline of waiting on the Lord, but my heart's desire is that we wait on the Lord with expectancy, knowing that God longs to tell us many things.

The voice of God in our lives is our daily bread. The word of God is that which hits our hearts. Like the men who were walking on the road to Emmaus with Jesus, while Jesus was speaking their hearts were burning. We live by every word that proceeds from His mouth. In the end it doesn't matter what man says about a certain situation, it's about what He says.

When He speaks everything changes. You are one word away from your greatest breakthrough.

THE EFFECTS OF GOD'S VOICE

- The voice of God creates. As we read in the first chapter of Genesis, the earth was without form and was void. Once the voice of God was released into the presence of God, creation took place.

  "The earth was without form, and void; and darkness was on the face of the deep. And the Spirit of God was hovering over the face of the waters. Then God said, 'Let there be light'; and there was light"

  ~ Gen. 1:2-3

  The universe and galaxies were created by God's word. The manifestation of the Kingdom happens at the declaration of the Word of God.

- The voice of God sustains. Our God is,

  "Upholding and maintaining and guiding and propelling the universe by His mighty word of power"

  ~ Heb. 1:3

The sun rises everyday because of God's living and active word. The rocks, trees, and stars are held together by His maintaining and sustaining powerful word. I believe if it weren't for the reality of God's living word in all that He has created, creation would in a moment explode into nothing. All sense of order would go and the earth would return to an empty void.

- The voice of God brings faith. "Faith comes by hearing, and hearing by the word of God" (Rom. 10:17). When we hear the *rhema,* life-giving word of God, faith is ignited in us.

"Then Jesus said to the centurion, 'Go! Let it be done just as you believed it would.' And his servant was healed at that moment"

~ Matt. 8:13

If you want to grow in your faith, then open your heart to hear His voice more. The key to great faith is great hearing.

- The voice of God destroys lies with truth. His Word comes and renews our mind into right thinking, equipping us to cast off the lies of the devil. His Word is truth, and truth is a person. Jesus came full of grace and truth (John 1:17). He is the way the truth and the life (John 14:6).

"And you shall know the truth, and the truth shall make you free"

~ John 8:32

God's word will always edify and build us up. His word never comes to lead us on a guilt trip or condemn us.

- The voice of God brings direction.

"They passed through the Phrygian and Galatian region, having been forbidden by the Holy Spirit to speak the word in Asia; and after they came to Mysia, they were trying to go into Bithynia, and the Spirit of Jesus did not permit them; and passing by Mysia, they came down to Troas. A vision appeared to Paul in the night: a man of Macedonia was standing and appealing to him, and saying, 'Come over to Macedonia and help us.' When he had seen the vision, immediately we sought to go into Macedonia, concluding that God had called us to preach the gospel to them"

~ Acts 16:6-10

- The voice of God renews our mind.

"Therefore I urge you, brethren, by the mercies of God, to present your bodies a living and holy sacrifice, acceptable to God, which is your spiritual service of worship. And do not be conformed to this world, but be transformed by the renewing of your mind, so that you may prove what the will of God is, that which is good and acceptable and perfect"

~ Rom. 12:1-2

- The voice of God commissions us into our God-ordained destinies.

"While they were worshiping the Lord and fasting, the Holy Spirit said, 'Set apart for me Barnabas and Saul for the work to which I have called them'"

~Acts 13:2

HAVING THE MIND OF CHRIST

"But we have the mind of Christ (the Messiah) and do hold the thoughts (feelings and purposes) of His heart"

~ 1 Cor. 2:16

The plans and purposes of God are not an unknown thing to God, and because we have the mind of Christ we have access to them. Our spirit man has been made perfect and in Christ knows all things. The Kingdom of God is inside us (Luke 17:21). Jesus Himself is the word made flesh, and the wonder of it all is that He lives inside of us (John 1:14; Col. 1:27). We have to realize that the Father loves us and longs to tell us all things. He is saying, "Call to me and I will answer you and tell you great and unsearchable things you do not know" (Jer. 33:3).

WHERE THE WORD COMES FROM

When we look at the effectiveness of a message someone gives, we must look primarily at the person who is giving it. Does that person have the authority to manifest the message and the power to enforce it? The way that we perceive the one who gives the message will determine how much faith we have in the ability to see that word fulfilled. How we see God will determine our faith in the ability to do the thing He said.

58

For example, say you can run 100 meters in 11 seconds. While you are training a six-year-old comes up to you and says, "You can do this. I know you can run this 100 meters in less than 10 seconds," you will be encouraged, but not in a big way. Now imagine, instead of the six year old, the fastest runner in the world came up to you and said, "You can do it. I have seen you run. I myself have done this, this will be easy for you." You would have incredible motivation to break the 10-second barrier because of the runner's encouragement. How much more will you be inspired when the maker of all things says you can do a certain thing? He believes in us more than we could ever know, and He knows us better than we could ever know ourselves. He loves to take "the weak things of the world to confound the things which are mighty" (1 Cor. 1:27).

In all this why do we not believe everything God has said? I believe it is because we do not have an accurate perception of who it is that gives the message. Doubt comes in when we have a poor perception of credibility of the one giving the word. This is why the message that God is good is such a needed word in the body of Christ today. When we realize how good and credible He really is, all doubt will fly away.

PETER'S BREAKTHROUGH

When we look at the story of Peter walking on water we have to ask the question, how did Peter walk on water? Was it his own internal faith? Or was it in how he saw Jesus, the one calling him out to walk on water?

"When the disciples saw Him walking on the sea, they were terrified, and said, 'It's a ghost!' And they cried out in fear. But immediately Jesus spoke to them, saying, 'Take courage, it is I; do not be afraid.'

Peter said to Him, 'Lord, if it is You, command me to come to You on the water.' And He said, 'Come!' And Peter got out of the boat, and walked on the water and came toward Jesus. But seeing the wind, he became frightened, and beginning to sink, he cried out, 'Lord, save me!' Immediately Jesus reached out his hand and took hold of him, and said to him, 'You of little faith, why did you doubt?' When they got into the boat, the wind stopped. And those who were in the boat worshiped Him, saying, 'You are certainly God's Son!' "

~ Matt. 14:26-33

In the midst of this incredibly terrifying situation, Peter asked Jesus if he could walk on water with Him. Peter knew, from living his day-to-day life with the Messiah, that if Jesus demonstrated something, He both expected and encouraged him to replicate it. In this situation, Peter knew that he needed the word from the Lord. One word from Jesus will overcome any obstacle. His line of thought was, "If Jesus said I can do it and He has done it, then I can do it."

God's word is always greater than our situation. No matter how contradicting our situations are to God's word, if He said something, it is possible. We are called to look at the one who gave the word, not the circumstance surrounding the word. Jesus stands on the other side of the impossibility of what He said we can do and calls us to walk into the impossible because He is there. Jesus never wants to save us from the waves and wind, He wants us to walk on them with the power of the living Word, which is Jesus the living Word made flesh.

THE ROMAN CENTURION

Another example we could look at would be the Centurion who asked Jesus to heal his valued slave. This Roman officer took Jesus at his word, and his view of Jesus unleashed an incredible measure of faith. "Just say the word from where you are and my servant will be healed," was the request of this Gentile Roman officer (Luke 7:7). His faith was in direct response to the way he viewed the Lord. He believed that Jesus had power over time and space. The Centurion also understood authority because he had it; he could just tell a soldier to do something and he would do it. The Centurion not only understood earthly authority, but spiritual authority too. He could see that if Jesus just said the word, the unseen angelic soldiers would fulfill His command. And because of this understanding of authority, Jesus stood amazed, remarking that He hadn't once seen faith like this in all of Israel (Luke 7:9).

Who Do You Say I Am?

It comes down to this question Jesus asked His disciples, "Who do you say I am?" (Matt. 16:15). Your perception of Him will determine the gateway through which He manifests. Author A. W. Tozer writes,

"What comes into your mind when you think about God? From this answer we could accurately determine the spiritual future of that individual."

(Tozer 1)

When God says something to us, we have the choice to believe it or deny the possibility of it. God is faithful.

"Though the fig tree should not blossom and there be no fruit on the vines, though the yield of the olive should fail and the fields produce no food, though the flock should be cut off from the fold and there be no cattle in the stalls, yet I will exult in the Lord, I will rejoice in the God of my salvation"

~ Hab. 3:17-18

God is big and He is our Father who loves us. Let us lift our heads and hear the voice of our Father. He is the living Word that abides in us. His voice is not far off, but He is the still small voice inside of us. All it takes is a whisper from heaven and everything changes.

5

SPIRITUAL SENSES: 1-2

INTRODUCTION

As we take a look at spiritual senses we must understand that they are available to every Christian. Christ has His home in us and therefore we are called to operate out of the spiritual senses of Christ. Although we have access to these senses, we may not be operating in them yet, so we need to move into these areas. We have become one with Christ, like being Siamese twins with Him, inseparable from birth.

Whatever Christ is able to taste we can taste. Whatever He smells we can smell. Whatever He feels, we can feel. Our hearts need to awaken to these possibilities.

The world of the supernatural and the natural are both real and in existence right now. These two worlds are often in close interaction with each other. The spiritual supernatural world has an incredible effect on the natural realm, and often the natural realm is a reflection of what's happening in the spiritual realm. Human acts of obedience or disobedience have an incredible effect on the spiritual realm. When we as children of God partner with God to shift spiritual atmospheres over countries and regions it will in turn change the atmosphere and situations, and the natural will be lined up with the Kingdom of heaven.

5 NATURAL SENSES / 5 SPIRITUAL SENSES

Every normal human being has the ability to operate using five natural senses, which are the ability to see, touch, taste, smell, and hear. When an individual is awakened to the spiritual supernatural realm, they enter into a whole new world of existence. Just as a human being needs their five natural senses in operation to explore this natural existence, so too does the child of God need their spiritual senses in operation to explore the spiritual world that God has invited us into.

MATURING OUR SENSES

For the most part these spiritual senses are matured and grown into.

"For though by this time you ought to be teachers, you have need again for someone to teach you the elementary principles of the oracles of God, and you have come to need milk and not solid food. For everyone who partakes only of milk is not accustomed to the word of righteousness, for he is an infant. But solid food is for the mature, who because of practice have their senses trained to discern good and evil"

~ Heb. 5:12-14

The operation of these senses in our lives gives us the ability to discern both good and evil, and the more we use them the greater their sensitivity and accuracy will be.

In the natural our senses excite and thrill us. They give us joy and pleasure. Imagine peering into the Grand Canyon while the sun is rising on a cloudless day, or listening to the harmonic sound that emanates from the New York Philharmonic Orchestra.

But these God-given senses are also given to protect us from all sorts of danger. The ability to smell is greatly appreciated before you pour month-old sour milk into your freshly brewed cup of coffee, as is having the ability to see a five-ton truck approaching you at 70 miles an hour.

So it is with our spiritual senses. God has given them for our joy and pleasure and for our protection. When we encounter the spiritual realm we need to be able to discern what is of God and how to partner with it, and what is of the demonic realm and how to defuse it, or at times ignore it.

TUNING INTO THE RIGHT STATION

Take for example an FM radio signal. On that FM signal there are many radio frequencies. Some offer amazing music stations and others not so amazing music stations. In the same way we need to tune our spiritual ears into the signal of heaven. Heaven's signal is pure and encouraging. While listening to it we are infused with peace and love.

Psychics and witch doctors use a variety of different mediums to enter the spiritual world. We as Christians only have one medium and that is Jesus. Our encounters will be in a safe place if our journey into this supernatural world is with heaven as our home, and Jesus as our heart's desire.
Jesus should be the center of everything. If He is not the center, then ask yourself who is.

"The Son is the image of the invisible God, the firstborn over all creation. For in him, all things

*were created: things in heaven and on earth,
visible and invisible, whether thrones or powers or
rulers or authorities; all things have been created
through him and for him. He is before all things,
and in him all things hold together"*

~ Col. 1:15-17

PURPOSE FOR OUR SPIRITUAL SENSES

Our spiritual senses are designed for us to encounter
our heavenly home. God has given us the ability to
touch, smell, see, taste, and hear heaven. We are not
called to predominantly interact with the demonic in
second heaven affairs. We are called to set our "minds
on things above, not on earthly things" because we
"have been raised up with Christ... where Christ is,
seated at the right hand of God" (Col. 3:1-2).

The Apostle Paul gives us an incredible introduction to what I believe is one of his third heaven,
throne rooms encounters.

*"I know a man in Christ who fourteen years ago –
whether in the body I do not know, or out of the
body I do not know, God knows – such a man was
caught up to the third heaven. And I know how
such a man – whether in the body or apart from
the body I do not know, God knows – was caught*

up into Paradise and heard inexpressible words, which a man is not permitted to speak."

In this encounter Paul's experience was so real to him that he could not discern if it was his natural senses experiencing paradise/heaven (in the body) or his spiritual senses (out of body), or if his actual body got taken to heaven or just his spirit man. Heaven is real and we have been made alive with Christ and raised up to be seated with Him in heavenly places (Eph. 2:5-6). So in a sense we are living in two places at the same time, on earth and in heaven. We are citizens of both heaven and of earth, so we have dual citizenship.

While Jesus was on earth He modeled how Christians are able to operate from heaven to earth. He taught us to pray, "Thy Kingdom come, Thy will be done in earth, as it is in heaven" (Matt. 6:10). We are called to declare and see the manifestation of heavenly realities on this earth. God has given us spiritual senses to perceive things in heaven and then enforce them on earth as God's chosen ambassadors. There will be a greater more accurate demonstration of God's Kingdom here on earth when we have our senses trained and matured to perceive what the Father is doing in heaven. So let's take a look at these God-given spiritual senses.

SEEING IN THE SPIRIT:
THE FATHER LOVES THE SON AND SHOWS HIM ALL THINGS

In these days God is awaking the sense of sight in many children of God. The operation of this sense is often called the seer gift because the person sees visions either when they are awake or sleeping.

"It will come about after this that I will pour out My Spirit on all mankind; and your sons and daughters will prophesy, your old men will dream dreams, your young men will see visions"

~ Joel 2:28

If we look at the life of Jesus, He placed a great importance on being able to see in the spiritual realm, especially seeing what he saw His Father doing.

"Truly, truly, I say to you, the Son can do nothing of Himself, unless it is something He sees the Father doing; for whatever the Father does, these things the Son also does in like manner. For the Father loves the Son, and shows Him all things that He Himself is doing; and the Father will show Him greater works than these, so that you will marvel. For just as the Father raises the dead and

gives life, even so the Son also gives life to whom He wishes."

~ John 5:19-21

Wow! That is amazing. This was the secret of Jesus' ministry. Whatever Jesus saw the Father doing Jesus manifested. Seeing in the spirit was so important to Jesus that He based the success of His entire ministry on it. Jesus knew that if He saw what the Father was doing in heaven then He could bring heaven to earth.

We are now one with Christ, co-equal heirs with Him. Whatever we see the Father doing, we can manifest. The question is, "Father what are you doing in heaven right now?" Because if we can see it, then we can declare it and see it manifested. What really blows my mind away in this Scripture is that because the Father loves us, He is willing to show us all things! In God there are no secrets and His heart's desire is to tell us everything about anything. We need to come to the place where we believe our Father really knows everything and He wants to tell us amazing things.

LESSONS FROM THE LIFE OF WILLIAM BRANHAM

The 1950's healing revivalist William Branham moved profoundly in the seer realm. Before meetings and in everyday life, God would give him through visions the exact proceedings of the day. He would see the forthcoming events and know exactly what to do and when to do it. William was known for the bizarre miracles God worked through him. His success was because he simply mimicked what he saw the Father doing in heaven.

THOSE WHO ARE WITH US ARE MORE THAN THOSE THAT ARE WITH THEM

I believe that God has called us to see in both realms. The spiritual realm is becoming more real to us than the air we breathe. I have not arrived there, but I know that across the world there are an increasing number of believers who are seeing clearer than ever before. God is no respecter of persons; what He will do for one He will do for another.

God's agenda for us is not that we would be impressed by the demonic and what they are doing but to see and be amazed by what He is doing. In 2 Kings 6 we read of the story of King Aram's plot to capture Elisha the prophet. King Aram had repeatedly tried to capture the King of Israel, but without success. Unbeknownst to him Elisha was prophetically warning the King of Israel of King Aram's plans. Finally the King of Aram found out the reason for his failed attempts to capture the King of Israel. Enraged he sent horses and chariots to capture Elisha, and they came by night and surrounded the city where Elisha was staying. In the morning Elisha's servant was extremely frightened at the impending danger.

"And his servant said to him, 'Alas, my master! What shall we do?' So he [Elisha] answered, 'Do not fear, for those who are with us are more than those who are with them.' And Elisha prayed, and said, 'Lord, I pray, open his eyes that he may see.' Then the Lord opened the eyes of the young man, and he saw. And behold, the mountain was full of horses and chariots of fire all around Elisha. So when the Syrians came down to him, Elisha prayed to the Lord, and said, 'Strike this people, I pray, with blindness.' And He struck them with blindness according to the word of Elisha."

~ 2 Kings 6:15-17

Everyday millions around the world are faced with incredible difficulties and fear grips them with the reality of their situations. In all this, there is a God who is for them and not against them. What a marvelous gift it is to see in the spirit that those who are with us are more than those who are against us. He wants our eyes to be open to see the angelic beings that He has sent to us to help us.

"Are not all angels ministering spirits sent to serve those who will inherit salvation?"

~ Heb. 1:14

74

Angels are helping us to bring the reality of heaven into our situations. God's desire is for us to see heaven, the angelic, living creatures, and many other things. There are things that God wants to show and tell us, heavenly things that we have no paradigm for.

"I have spoken to you of earthly things and you do not believe; how then will you believe if I speak of heavenly things?"

~ John 3:12

SEEING THROUGH THE EYES OF A CHILD

Our prayer should be that the eyes our heart may be enlightened, like Paul prayed for the Ephesians (Eph. 1:18). In the Greek, *"eyes of your heart,"* means imagination. God literally uses our imagination to imprint the visual realities of the spirit realm. He paints spiritual realities on the canvas of our heart's imaginations. Whether we see in the spirit with our eyes open or with our eyes closed makes no difference. What matters is the state of our heart.

"But Jesus called for them, saying, 'Permit the children to come to Me, and do not hinder them, for the kingdom of God belongs to such as these. Truly I say to you, whoever does not receive the kingdom of God like a child will not enter it at all.' "

~ Luke 16:17

75

To become like a child in your heart is one of the most important keys to seeing in the spirit. There are things that the Father wants to show us but unless we have the heart attitude of a child we will never see them.

GROWING IN OUR ABILITY TO SEE

One of the problems of operating in the seer realm is that when people see a detailed event in a vision they might assume that the manifestation of the event will happen immediately or very soon. Don't ever assume that what you see will take place in the next week or month. People who interpret the timing to be soon for themselves or another person can be hurt or left despondent when it doesn't happen soon because they did not realized the fulfillment was meant for a later time.

My advice to prophetic people who see visions is to ask questions. Ask God for the specific time, date, and place of the upcoming events you see. He may or may not reveal the timing to you, but it is a good idea to ask. If you are relaying a vision to someone else and you don't know the timing of what you saw, be honest and tell them you don't know the timing. The Lord wants us to grow in our ability to see in the spirit, He is a good God who wants to give us more. If you are only seeing black and white you can ask God to show you color. If you are seeing vague objects ask him to show you every detail, and then when you are finished with the vision or dream write them down.

TOUCHING IN THE SPIRIT: TOUCHING THE DIVINE

When we talk about touching in the spirit, we are predominately talking about touching things that are divine and heavenly. One of the signs that we know we are touching the heavenly realities is when we feel the divine surge of heavenly virtue and glory in our natural bodies. When we physically feel the glorious presence of God in a meeting, we are touching with our spiritual sense the glory of God.

REVELATION LEADS TO MANIFESTATION

On the other hand, I also want to make it clear that you don't need to feel something to know that something is happening. For example, there are many testimonies of people being healed without even feeling anything. Only after they tried to do something they could not do, they discovered that they were healed. In the same way we also don't need to feel God's love for us to believe He loves us. Experiencing God's love often happens when we have a revelation of how much He loves us.

God's love is in many ways different from the world's. We are brought up in a world that functions out of conditional love. If I take you out to coffee, I expect you to buy my coffee next time. Often the mindset is, if I scratch your back you should scratch my back. This is what the world thinks love is, and in a sense it believes we need to work and perform for love. People's love for each other is based on how other people perform for them, and how they meet their needs.

GOD'S UNCONDITIONAL LOVE

But God's love for us is unconditional. It is not based on our performance for Him, but on His performance on our behalf. The revelation that God loves us one hundred percent all the time is vital. He does not love us more if we live purer lives and do great exploits for Him. In the same way He does not love us less if we mess up and drift away from following Him. His love for us does not waver; it is constant and unchangeable. We are the object of His affection and He delights in loving us. That being said we do not need to feel His love in order to know that He loves us. When Jesus died on the cross the physical veil in the tabernacle that separated man from God was ripped from top to bottom. There is now no distance or space between God and man. He is Immanuel, God with us. He is closer than the air we breathe. He has now made man a walking tabernacle of His presence and glory.

There is no end to how much an individual can touch and feel and know God's presence. God is looking for individuals who will test the extremes of how much one person can carry His glory. D.L. Moody, who was used powerfully by God and saw thousands saved in the U.S. and Britain, said, *"There is no end to how much God can use a man who is fully His."*

EXPERIENCING HIS TOUCH

Touching and feeling the person of the Holy Spirit is an exhilarating experience. An individual may feel a vast array of sensations like fire, peace, electricity, coolness, and numbness. When I am in God's presence my hands become numb or burn like they are on fire. But for every individual it is different. These physical feelings in the natural reflect what your spirit man is feeling too.

KNOWING HOW HE TOUCHES YOU

While you are ministering it is vitally important to take careful notice of what you are feeling on your body. For example, God may want to heal someone and suddenly you feel God's presence like heat or numbness all over you hands when you are close to a particular individual or group of people. Or maybe you feel a surge of glory down the one side of your body, indicating the possible arrival of an angelic presence. When the glory of God comes into a room, I may at times feel a weight all over me, especially on my hands. David writes,

"O God, You are my God; I shall seek You earnestly; my soul thirsts for You, my flesh yearns for You"

~ Ps. 63:1

Here we see David's flesh yearning for God. I believe that David's natural physical body became so accustomed to the presence of God after spending hours a day worshipping God that his soul, flesh, and spirit longed to be in the presence of God again. His very flesh had developed a memory of being in God's presence and it yearned for the glory of the Lord.

DETERMINING THE SPIRITUAL CLIMATE

Most people feel spiritual atmospheres, and they are not even aware of it. When walking into different stores you can feel, with your spirit man, the spiritual atmosphere. Primarily this spiritual atmosphere is determined by what atmosphere the owner or manager (authority head) is carrying. If you walk into someone's house for example, almost immediately if you are open to the environment you will sense the spiritual state of the individuals who live there. For example the atmosphere could be full of joy, love, and warmth, or sadness, depression, and coldness. In all this we need to develop an acute awareness of our spiritual sense of touch. This greatly helps us in our journey of discovering what is of God and what is of the devil.

WE GET TO SET THE ATMOSPHERE

We, as children of God, are walking revivalists. We carry the atmosphere of heaven because we are seated in heavenly places. What is the atmosphere of heaven like? The atmosphere of heaven is a place where the fruits of the Holy Spirit are fully manifested. In other words, the fruit of the Holy Spirit is the atmosphere of heaven.

"But the fruit of the Spirit is love, joy, peace, forbearance, kindness, goodness, faithfulness, gentleness and self control"

~ Gal. 5:22-23

When you encounter through your spiritual sense of touch other demonic atmospheres you can partner with God and release the fruit of the Holy Spirit. All you need to do is release the opposite of what you are encountering. If you encounter anger then release peace. If you feel fear then release love because "perfect love drives out fear" (1 John 4:18). If you encounter depression then release joy. Where there is frustration release patience. The fruit of the Holy Spirit will always trump any demonic atmosphere you encounter. Whatever atmosphere you focus on will increase.

That is why the Bible says,
"Set your minds on things that are above, not on things that are on earth"

~ Col. 3:2

Wherever there is darkness, release light. Darkness is after all, just the absence of light. The light of who Jesus is fills the whole of heaven, and there is no need for a sun or moon (Rev. 21:23). This same Jesus has His habitation in us; therefore we carry the atmosphere of heaven wherever we go.

When the atmosphere of heaven is evident in a place or person, then the things of heaven begin to manifest on earth fulfilling the will of God, which is "on earth as it is in heaven" (Matt. 6:10). We have the authority to enforce heaven's atmosphere because we are ambassadors of heaven (2 Cor. 5:20).

One of the ways we can do this is by declaring the fruit of the Holy Spirit. When you make these declarations the Kingdom of God invades this earth. The Bible says,

"You will also decree a thing, and it will be established for you; and light will shine on your ways"

~ Job 22:28

The great Holy Spirit lives inside you. You are a temple of the Holy Spirit. Let the atmosphere of the fruit of the Holy Spirit come forth from your life. Arise and shine, and let God in you change the world around you. Let your inner world change your outer world.

TOUCHING THE HEM OF HIS GARMENT

Let us look at the story of the woman with the issue of blood, who reached out and touched the hem of Jesus' garment and was immediately healed (Mark 5:21-34). We see a powerful image of what it looks like to touch Jesus using our spirit man. This woman who was subject to bleeding for twelve years reached out with a touch of faith and received what she was looking for.

"After hearing about Jesus, she came up in the crowd behind Him and touched His cloak. For she thought, 'If I just touch His garments, I will get well.' Immediately the flow of her blood was dried up, and she felt in her body that she was healed of her affliction. Immediately Jesus, perceiving in Himself that the power proceeding from Him had gone forth, turned around in the crowd and said, 'Who touched My garments?' And His disciples said to Him, 'You see the crowd pressing in on You, and You say, "Who touched Me?" ' And He looked around to see the woman who had done this. But the woman fearing and trembling, aware

of what had happened to her, came and fell down before Him and told Him the whole truth. And He said to her, 'Daughter, your faith has made you well; go in peace and be healed of your affliction.'"

~ Mark 5:27-34

When Jesus said, "Who touched My garments?" the word "garments" in Greek is the same word used for "wings" found in Malachi 4. ("the sun of righteousness will rise with healing in its' wings" Malachi. 4:2).

Jesus was not delusional like His disciples thought when He asked the question, "Who touched Me?" His question had no relation to the natural sensations he was feeling as the crowd was pressing all around Him. He felt by His spiritual senses that someone had touched Him with the expectation of being healed. He felt someone touching Him with faith and drawing out healing virtue.

TOUCHED WITH FAITH

When this woman reached out and touched Jesus, it was not a natural touch of desperation, or even a touch of curiosity. She touched Jesus with a touch of faith from her spirit man. Her faith in Christ's ability to heal literally drew healing virtue out of the Messiah. Her faith was not in her faith but in God's faithfulness. The many people pushing in all around her did not distract her. Instead her focus was on Jesus, and the crowd faded into the background as she reached out to touch Him.

This woman was risking her very life just to be there. Jewish law prohibited her from being in contact out in the open with other clean Jews, especially in a crowd that size. By Jewish law the unclean person would be subject to the death penalty, probably by stoning. When we see Jesus in all His faithfulness we are infused with faith.

MINISTERING FROM OUR SPIRIT MAN

We are called to worship God in spirit and in truth (John 4:24). I have observed services where some people are getting powerfully touched by God and other people in the same meeting are not feeling God's presence. Our hunger and faith sensitize our spirit man to feel and experience the presence of God. God's presence can be powerful in a meeting but like in the story above you can be so close to God, right in His presence, even touching Him, but not have a powerful spiritual experience. When we learn not just to sing songs and pray from our head, but to worship and adore Him with our spirit man, singing from our hearts, with our desire, affection, and focus on the lover of our souls, we will discover a whole new world of experiencing the tangible presence of God.

6

SPIRITUAL SENSES: 3-5

SMELLING IN THE SPIRIT:
OUR NEED TO SMELL IN THE SPIRIT

Now let's look at smelling in the spirit. Its important to understand that smelling in the spirit and tasting in the spirit are closely interlinked. Just like in the natural if you smell something amazing, like freshly baked cookies, your salivary glands go crazy and you can almost taste them, so it is in the spirit. What we smell is closely linked to what we are about to taste. In my opinion, across the body of Christ today the development of these two senses is greatly needed. While we are having heavenly encounters our heart's desire should be not only to see heaven, hear heaven, and feel heaven, but also to smell heaven. Can you imagine the unique smells found in heaven, especially the fragrance emanating from the very throne room?

YOUR NAME IS LIKE PERFUME POURED OUT

In Song of Solomon we read,

"Let him kiss me with the kisses of his mouth — for your love is more delightful than wine. Pleasing is the fragrance of your perfumes; your name is like perfume poured out. No wonder the young women love you!"

~ Song of Solomon 1:2-3

To better understand this Scripture, it helps to understand that men in Solomon's day rarely bathed. They used ointments to keep their skin from drying out and to give them a pleasing fragrance. This young woman was captivated and drawn to Solomon's intoxicating fragrance. Both his cologne and the godly reputation his name held enraptured her. His name spoke of his character, virtue, and heritage.

Song of Solomon in many ways is a prophetic image of Christ and His bride the church. Christ Himself has a particular unique fragrance. Imagine the release of this supernatural heavenly fragrance as all the living creatures, elders, and angels bow down to worship Jesus. So too, when we the bride of Christ rise up and worship Him who is worthy, the one who has the name above all other names. Will not the place of our worship be filled with the supernatural fragrance of heaven? God's desire and plan has always been for us to experience the realities of heaven here on earth.

THE SMELL OF OUR WORSHIP AND PRAYER

The Bible says that our worship and prayers release unique fragrances.

In Revelation 8:4-5 we read,
"the smoke of the incense, with the prayers of the saints, ascended before God from the angel's hand. Then the angel took the censer, filled it with fire from the altar, and threw it to the earth. And there were noises, thundering's, lightning's, and an earthquake."

When we look at the Old Testament tabernacle, the incense always represented the prayers of Israel. What do these incense offerings of prayer smell like? In worship what do our songs of adoration smell like? Perhaps they smell like the room when Mary anointed Jesus for His burial (John 12). The whole room was filled with the fragrance of the perfume. When we worship Him giving Him a sacrifice of praise and worship, the place where we meet is filled with a unique supernatural fragrance.

I have been in a number of meetings where people in the meeting suddenly smelled the supernatural fragrance of heaven. They remarked that it was the most beautiful thing they ever smelled. Some said it smelled like a certain flower and some could not identify it precisely.

We as Christians have a particular spiritual fragrance, which we are continually releasing.

"For we are a fragrance of Christ to God among those who are being saved; to the one an aroma from death to death, to the other an aroma from life to life"

~ 2 Cor. 2:15-16

What is this fragrance? It is the "sweet aroma of the knowledge of Him in every place" (2 Cor. 2:14). This fragrance is released whenever and wherever we go. We are a continuous beautiful fragrance unto the Lord and the world around us. A smell will either draw someone towards you or repel them from you.

METAL DISSOLVING

The supernatural sense of smell can also be used with the gifts of words of knowledge, healing, and miracles. Today God is blowing our minds with what He is doing on the face of the earth. One of the most amazing signs and wonders is God taking away metal from people's bodies. I honor doctors, and they do their best with what they can do. We are seeing God, the great physician, heal physical conditions that needed the metal replacement.

On one occasion my friend Chuck Parry was in the Bethel Healing Rooms when suddenly he smelled metal burning. He started walking around the different rooms searching for where the smell was coming from. Finally he realized that God was telling him that He wanted to melt metal in a person's body, and him smelling metal burning was a word of knowledge, or you could say a smell of knowledge. Finally he came into a totally different room and discovered which person it was by following the smell of knowledge. A young man had two metal plates with eight screws on each side holding his jaws together and he could only open his jaw a little bit. God completely melted the metal in his jaw and he was able to open his mouth wide.

DEMONIC AWARENESS

The spiritual sense of smell can be used to even warn us of the demonic. Just like the warning bells in our mind would immediately go off if we were to walk around a corner and smell a horrific scent, our spiritual sense of smell can alert us to something that is not right. I have entered into demonic situations and the spiritual scent released from demons at times have smelled horrific. The devil is also called Beelzebub "Lord of the flies," and where there are demons there is always death. We as believers have been called to smell in the spirit what is of life, and what is of death and choose to partner with life.

TASTING IN THE SPIRIT:
THE BANQUET FEAST

God sends out an invitation to, "taste and see that the Lord is good" (Ps. 34:8). It is possible for us to taste of the Lord's goodness in the land of the living. God has said, "open wide your mouth and I will fill it" (Ps. 81:10). His desire is that we would be filled and satisfied with the bounty of His house. "He has brought me to his banquet hall, and his banner over me is love" (Song of Sol. 2:4). He has a lavish banquet feast for us, we are called to indulge ourselves in the finest of foods He has for us.

In Song of Solomon the author used figurative language to describe two individuals' love for each other. These individuals correlated their sensual desires and passion to the pleasure found in eating sweet foods like fruit and honey (Song of Sol. 2:3, 4:11). In our journey of enjoying God and feasting at the table of His love we can, with our spiritual sense of taste, actually taste the Lord's goodness.

FEASTING ON HIS GOODNESS

During times of worship and prayer individuals may taste of heavenly delights. Some may taste honey in their mouth or stomach and others may taste wine as they are getting filled with God's glorious joy. He has laid out an extravagant feast before us, and His desire is for us to experience the tastes of heaven.

God's open invitation still stands,

"Come, all you who are thirsty, come to the waters; and you who have no money, come, buy and eat! Come, buy wine and milk without money and without cost"

~ Isa. 55:1

TASTING OF GOD'S LIVING WORD

During Ezekiel's vision God told him to eat the scroll, and to go and speak to Israel the word of God. When he ate it he remarked, "it tasted as sweet as honey in my mouth" (Ezek. 3:3).

In the same way John the Revelator ate heavenly things,

"I took the little book out of the angel's hands and ate it, and in my mouth it was sweet as honey; and when I had eaten it, my stomach was made bitter"

~ Rev. 10:10

The psalmist says about God's Word,

"How sweet are Your words to my taste, sweeter than honey to my mouth!"

~ Ps. 119:103

Tasting a message, whether it is heard on a Sunday morning in church, read in the Word, or received by a friend or prophetic stranger, is vitally important. Ask yourself if the message tastes sweet and pleasant like honey or like death, guilt, and condemnation. Does it leave a good or bad taste in your mouth? The answer to this question most likely will reveal the source of the word and whether you should keep or discard it.

HEARING IN THE SPIRIT:
HIS SHEEP SHALL HEAR HIS VOICE

Lastly, let's look at hearing in the spirit. I have talked quite a bit about hearing God's voice already in The Voice of God chapter, so in this section I will share about ways to recognize God's voice and hearing sounds in heaven.

I believe that as Christians we called to hear the voice of God. We are the sheep of His pasture, and we are designed to hear His voice (John 10:27). Believing that we can hear His voice is a giant leap in the right direction. The next step is to recognize it when He speaks to us.

"The words of the Lord are pure words; as silver tried in a furnace on the earth, refined seven times"

~ Ps. 12:6

In God, there are many languages through which He may speak to us. It may come through hearing the word on Sunday, interaction with other people, nature, road signs, books, movies, songs, angels, and even through our dream life. God is a creative God. He loves to use creative and innovative ways to speak to us. Sometimes God likes to switch up the way that He speaks to us because He wants to grow our ability to hear His voice. So if you're not hearing God's voice then it's possible He is speaking to you in another way.

HEARING HEAVENLY THINGS

Hearing in the spirit is not limited to the ability to hear God's voice. In the heavenlies there are many sounds and songs that God longs for us to hear. While we have heavenly encounters there is no greater thrill than hearing the sounds of heaven.

Paul's talks about his third heaven encounter, he,

"was caught up into paradise, and he heard utterances beyond the power of man to put into words, which man is not permitted to utter"

~ 2 Cor. 12:4

Paul heard things that are indescribable; to try and describe them would be an injustice. There are sounds, rhythms, beats, melodies, and new songs that are totally unique to heaven. I believe all of heaven waits in anticipation for people on earth to discover and create the sounds that are already in existence in heaven.

WHAT DOES HEAVEN SOUND LIKE?

Heaven is not a quiet place; it is actually pretty loud at times, especially around the throne room of God. "Out from the throne came flashes of lightning and rumblings and peals of thunder" (Rev. 4:5). There are the twenty-four elders falling prostrate before the King worshipping the Lamb, casting down their crowns. The living creatures are crying out day and night, "Holy, holy, holy is the Lord God Almighty (Omnipotent), Who was and Who is and Who is to come" (Rev. 4:8). It says that thousands and thousands of elders, living creatures, and angels around the throne are saying with a loud voice, "Worthy is the Lamb that was slain to receive power and riches and wisdom and might and honor and glory and blessing" (Rev. 5:11-12). There are new songs being sung by the elders (Rev. 5:9), angels sounding loud trumpets, and saints as far as you can see dressed in white crying out, "Salvation to our God who sits on the throne, and to the Lamb" (Rev. 7:10).

EZEKIEL'S HEAVENLY ENCOUNTERS

While Ezekiel was having his heavenly encounter he clearly heard the sounds the living creatures were making.

"I also heard the sound of their wings like the sound of abundant waters as they went, like the voice of the Almighty, a sound of tumult like the sound of an army camp"

~ Ezek. 1:24-25

"And I heard the sound of the wings of the living beings touching one another and the sound of wheels beside them, even a great rumbling sound"

~ Ezek. 3:13

It is evident that during this vision Ezekiel's sense of hearing was awakened as he encountered heavenly realities, and so can ours.

Across the world today the children of God are hearing the sounds of heaven. Some people hear with their natural ears the songs of angels during times of worship (Jason Upton's Recording of song: Fly), while others hear with their spiritual ears. Regardless of whether people hear heaven with their natural or spiritual ears, one thing is for sure, God desires us to hear heaven's songs.

$$\boxed{7}$$

HEART OF GOD

COMPLETELY SURRENDERED TO HIM

God's desire is that we would have an understanding of His heart. For those that are willing to open up their hearts to God's heart, their lives will be forever transformed.

"The Lord's eyes keep on roaming throughout the earth, looking for those whose hearts completely

belong to him, so that he may strongly support them"

~ 2 Chron. 16:9

God is looking for hearts that are completely given over to Him. When hearts are completely given over to the creator of heaven and earth, they will get caught up into the reality of His heart.

The greatest thing you can give God is your heart. Your heart is your entire being; it is the core of who you are as a person. The Bible says it is the "wellspring of life" (Prov. 4:23). What would it look like to know God's heart, the heart from which all life flows out of? God is looking for fearless lovers that would give everything away in return for His heart. Our one desire should be to know God's heart, presence, love, and power.

THE PURSUIT OF HIS HEART

God never intended for us to know Him on an intellectual basis only. Some people only know about God's attributes but they have never felt God's emotions. They have never felt the joy that God has for people or the pain that grips His heart when they choose to deny Him. For many, God is an emotionless authoritarian figure, and not an emotional Father that loves them.

What good would it be to married to a person that you never experienced? Would it be true love if you never knew what their touch felt like? What if you spoke to them but they never spoke to you? What if they never expressed their love to you? Relationships are a two-way street. We are referred to as the bride of Christ...

REALLY KNOWING GOD / HOW THE GREEKS THINK

"*I want to know* Christ and experience the mighty power that raised him from the dead" (Phil. 3:10 *emphasis added*). Here we see that "to know" in Greek is the word *ginōskō*. In the original language it means to feel, perceive, and experientially and intimately know someone. In Hebraic culture, people would only say they knew about something if they experienced it. If you asked someone raised in a Hebraic culture whether they know about Canada and they had not been there before they would say, "No, I have no experience of that place." They have never met the people, eaten their food, or walked their streets. They would not know about Canada unless they had been there themselves. In contrast, the Western way of thinking is really different. People feel they know about something because they intellectually understand facts about it. God wants to grip our hearts so that we know Him, not only on an intellectual basis but on an experiential one.

Revelation in the Kingdom must always lead to manifestation. If the manifestation of the Kingdom is not evident in your life, somewhere on the journey your experience of God has just become head knowledge.

"But the people who know their God shall be strong, and carry out great exploits"

~Dan. 11:32

"He made known his ways to Moses, his acts to the people of Israel"

~ Ps. 103:7

Moses knew the ways of God, which included God's thoughts and desires. He knew God's heart and he spoke to God face to face, as a man speaks to a friend (Exod. 33:11). I believe because of this he followed the Lord all the days of his life. Israel on the other hand only knew the acts of God, which were the demonstrations of God's authority and power. They did not know God's heart like Moses. The result was that Israel was continuously led astray and did not follow God wholeheartedly.

God does not reveal His power with signs and wonders and miracles so that people will just know His power. Miracles are always meant to lead people to the miracle worker Himself. Demonstrations of the power of God should always lead us to a greater revelation of the heart of God, which is love. Healings were never only intended to just touch a body, but also to touch the person's soul (mind, will, and emotions). God's power will affect a person but His love will change a person forever. Why? "Love never fails" (1 Cor. 13:8).

LOVE IS OUR MESSAGE

The Bible does not say that God is power or authority. It says, "God is love" (1 John 4:8). To know the heart of God is to know His love. He lives in us and we are one with Him. This means we are one with His love, and because we are one with God we have His heart. We are in a perpetual encounter with the love of God.

"As the Father has loved me, so have I loved you. Now remain in my love"

~John 15:9

All the Father's love and desire is towards us. We are objects of His love and affection. Opening our hearts allows the love of God to affect our mind will and emotions.

GOD STRIPPING ME OF PERFORMANCE CHRISTIANITY

As I have previously mentioned in this book, for many years I related to God with a strong performance mentality. I felt if I wanted more of the heart of God, more power, and more favor I would need to perform to earn it. I thought if only I prayed and read my Bible more, God would love me more.

At that time I was living in Hong Kong, constantly praying and seeking God. But one day God said to me, "Ryan stop! Stop everything." I was startled by what I had heard. God then said, "Ryan stop praying, stop reading, stop fasting, and become an object of my love and affection. My desire for you is that you would experience the height, depth, and length of my love. But you can't perform to experience it."

These verses profoundly spoke to me:

"So that Christ may dwell in your hearts through faith; and that you, being rooted and grounded in love, may be able to comprehend with all the saints what is the breadth and length and height and depth, and to know the love of Christ which surpasses knowledge, that you may be filled up to all the fullness of God. "

~ Eph. 3:17-19

For the next month, I would lay on my bed as wave after wave of God's glorious love filled every fiber of my being. I encountered God's heart for me, and as I did my heart would swell with love for Him and others. Constantly I would hear God say, "Ryan you don't have to perform for my love."

Reading the Bible, praying, fasting, and worshiping are all incredible gifts from God to help us know Him more. But for me I saw them as tools for performance instead of tools for relationship. My desire now when I read, pray, fast, and worship is to get to know Him more. God needed to strip me of all my performance mindsets to show me His unconditional love.

CHANGING OUR HAVE TO'S TO WANT TO'S

Unconditional love means that God can't love you any more than He loves you right now. He didn't love you more when you did better, or any less when you messed up. He loves you 100% of the time. His love never fluctuates. God's love is not based on how much you read your Bible or how much you don't, or on how much you witness or how much you don't. A revelation of His unconditional love will change your have to's of performance to want to's of love.

ALL CONSUMING LOVE OF GOD

God's desire for us is that we would be caught up in divine romance with Him, and that we would know Him and be known by Him. He wants us to know what makes Him happy, what makes Him sad, what His dreams are, and what it is He is doing on the earth right now. The love of God will always open us up to divine purpose.

OPENING OUR HEARTS TO EXPERIENCE HIM

We have the heart of God because we are one with Him. Will we open our hearts to experience His heart? Our hearts are the wellspring of life. When our hearts connect to God's heart (wellspring of life) intimacy is birthed. To encounter the heart of God means we encounter the mind, emotions, and will of God.

The nature of God is that He loves to give you the desires of your heart (Ps. 37:4). He so desires to be with us that He took up residence inside of us. He desires for our hearts to encounter His heart. His dream was that we would live in the same home together and have constant communion. Our hearts are the garden that God wants to walk in.

GOING BACK TO THE GARDEN

The word "Eden" in Hebrew means "delight/pleasure." God's delight is for us to walk with Him together in the garden of our hearts, like Adam and Eve walked with Him in the beginning. In the garden we were made in the image of love because God is love, and now love itself lives in us. God's love is the love that every heart longs for, and the wonder of it all is that He now lives in us the saints of God. He is the longing of every heart.

Unfortunately, just like we can live in the same house as someone else and not acknowledge or take time to get to know them. So too, we can share the same room with God but never take the time to get to know Him.

WE HAVE BEEN MADE ONE WITH HIS HEART

The reality is that we can't get any closer to God than we are right now.

"But whoever is united with the Lord is one with him in spirit"

~ 1 Cor. 6:17

We still need to draw near to God, but I believe this looks like opening our hearts and turning our affections towards Him. Our greatest desire is to know the heart of God. When we know God's heart, then the eyes of our heart will be opened (Eph. 1:18). When this happens we will see as He sees and do as He does. We are divinely infused together with Christ, so let us open our hearts to receive the fullness of God's love for us.

Thank you for taking the time to read this book. I trust that the revelation and anointing in this book, has powerfully impacted and changed your life.

I pray over you Ephesians 1:17 - that the eyes of your heart would be opened, and spirit of revelation would infuse your being to know the full inheritance that is yours in Jesus. I pray that the revelation of who it is that lives in you, will catapult you into an adventure into the heart of God that is beyond your wildest dreams.

BIBLE TRANSLATIONS USED:
(All versions taken from biblegateway.com)

AMP
CEV
ESV
ISV
KJV
NASB
NIV
NKJV
NLT
NLV
WEB

REFERENCES USED:

1) Lake, John G. John G. Lake: His Life, His Sermons, His Boldness of Faith. Ft. Worth, TX: Kenneth Copeland Publications, 1994. Print.

2) Tozer, A. W. The Knowledge of the Holy: The Attributes of God, Their Meaning in the Christian Life. New York: Harper & Row, 1961. Print.

PROPHETIC
C R E A T I O N S

Inpiring prophetic art by Christian artists

propheticcreations.com

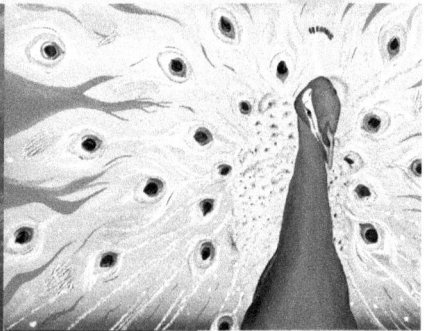

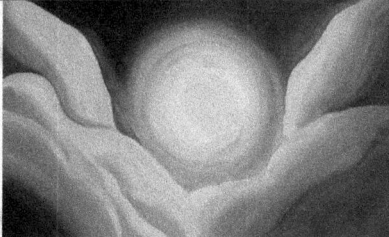

Our website is an online comunity of artists from around the world.
We believe Prophetic Art is inspirational creativity driven by a
desire to co-create with God. God's kingdom is powerfully
advancing through Prophetic Art, and our passion is to be used as
a platform for God to impact the nations of the world.

Visit propheticcreations.com

"It is with incredible delight that I write this. The power of this manual is not that it simply carries principals: it clearly carries theheart of the Prince. This generation needs an encounter with the Father's love. **Healing and miracles are simply an expression of God's heart towards His people.**"

Chris Gore
Director of Bethel Healing Rooms

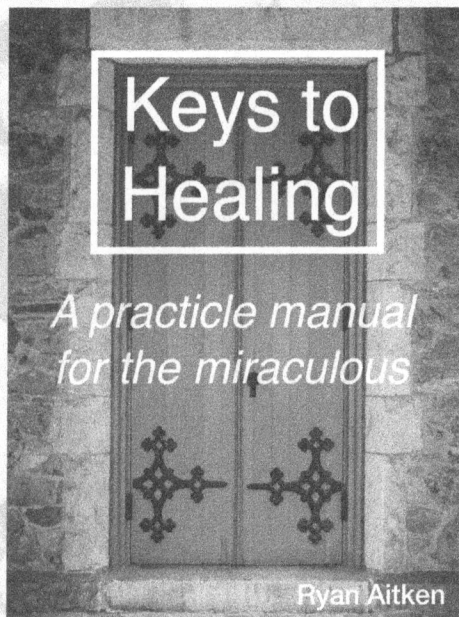

Keys to Healing

A practicle manual for the miraculous

Ryan Aitken

"Keys to Healing" is a practical manual full of revelation needed to develop a healing ministry. These **equipping keys** are used around the world to see bodies touched and healed in the name of Jesus. This manual also includes activation exercises and spaces to journal in response to questions.

When Jesus died on the cross He paid the full price for our bodies to be healed. For most of the church, **healing is our neglected inheritance**, and God is rising up a generation of radical believers that will take Him at His word. He is looking for people he can use to invade the impossible with great displays of His power.

Visit: spiritofrevivalministries.com to order a copy

www.ingramcontent.com/pod-product-compliance
Lightning Source LLC
Chambersburg PA
CBHW072355090426
42741CB00012B/3046